COLOR THRU HISTORY

The People of Early Civilization
Elementary Supplement

LEARN AND COLOR

Fulton, KY

Current and upcoming titles:

Learn and Color Nature Series

Medicinal Herbs

Freshwater Fish

Garden Edibles

Learn and Color Stained Glass Series

Landscapes & Seascapes

Fish & Fowl

Flowers

COLOR THRU HISTORY

Early Civilization

The Ancient World

The Middle Ages

The Renaissance and Reformation

The Industrial Revolution

The Modern Age

The Computer Age

Adam and Eve disobeyed God and ate the fruit.

9
6
9

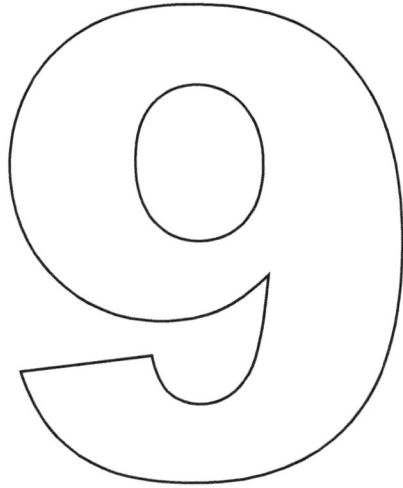

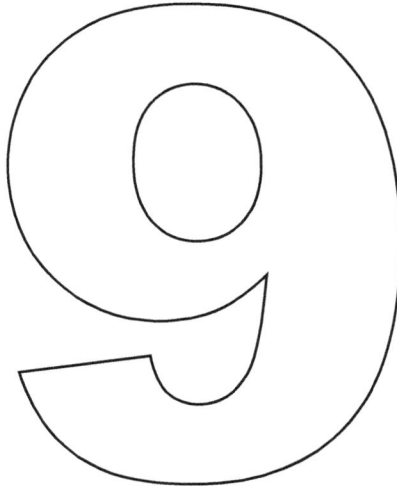

Methuselah lived to be 969 years old.

Noah built an ark to save his family and many animals from the Flood.
The rainbow is the sign of God's promise
to never flood the whole earth again.

Sargon the Great of Akkad was a great Mesopotamian king.

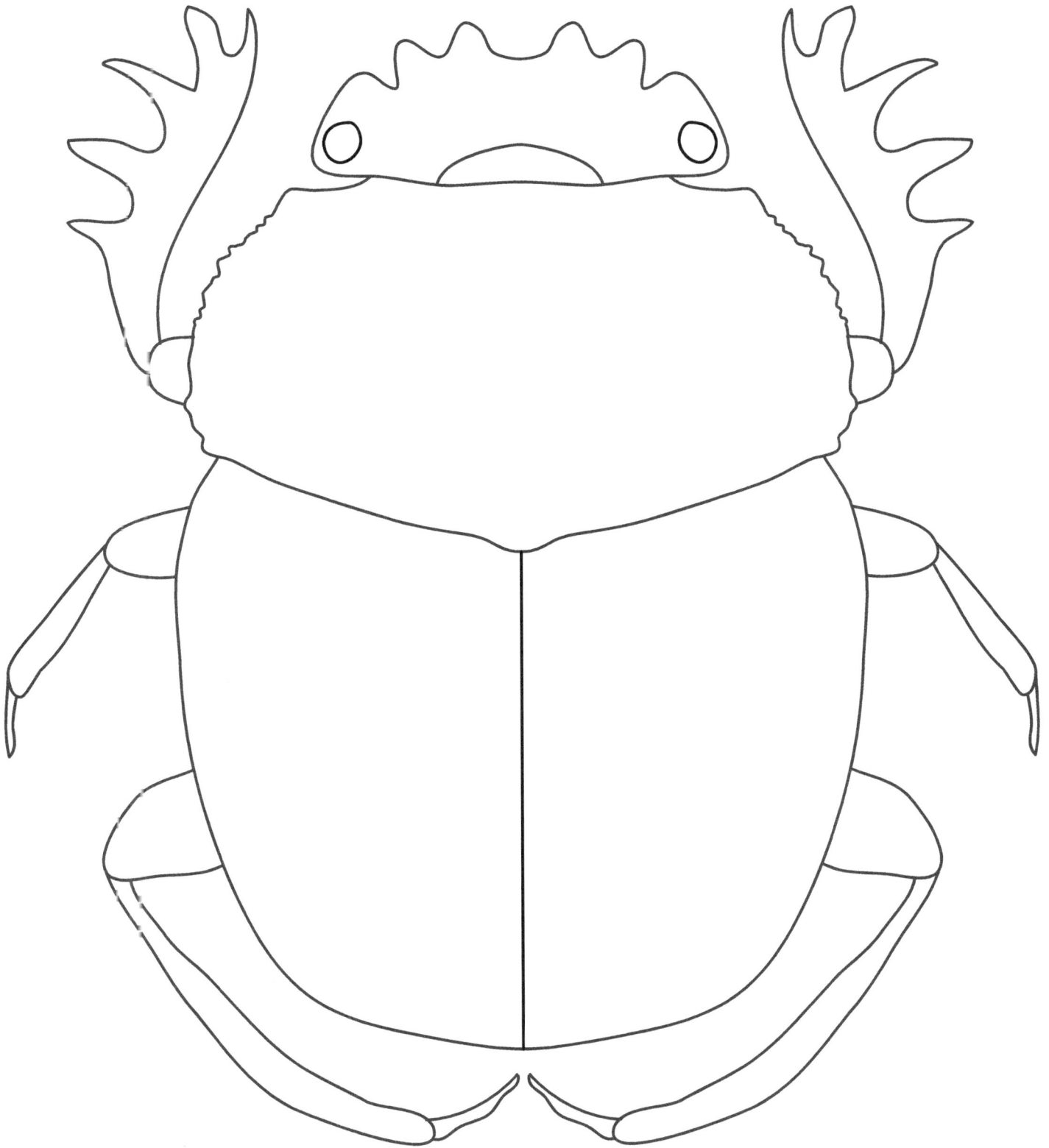

Imhotep designed of the Pyramid of Djoser.

I will bless those who bless you.

Abraham is known as the Father of Israel.

Hammurabi created the first set of laws.

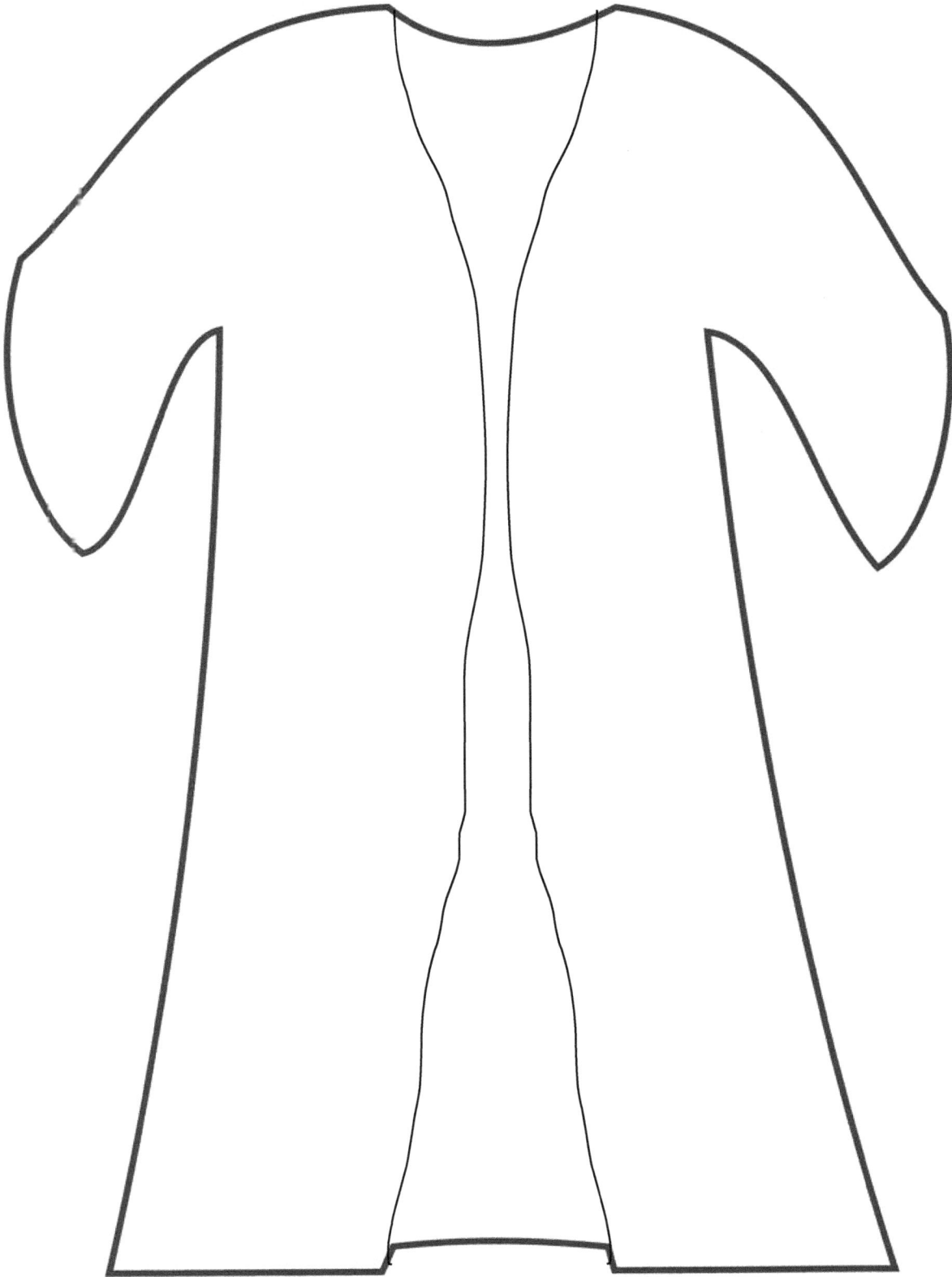

Joseph had a coat with lots of colors.
He saved his family from being hungry.

Hatshepsut was a King of Egypt.
She ruled Egypt longer than any other woman.

Thutmose III was King of Egypt.
He was called a Pharaoh.

God helped Moses free the Israelites from Egypt
and lead them to the Promised Land.

Amenhotep IV was an ancient Egyptian Pharaoh.
He and his wife Nefertiti worshipped the sun.
His son was Tutankhamun or King Tut.

Nefertiti was an Egyptian queen.
When the king died, she became ruler.

Ramesses II was known as Ramesses the Great.
He was king or pharaoh of Egypt.
His body is now on display in the Egyptian Museum.

David was King of Israel. God called David a man after His own heart.

Guard your heart

Solomon was the wisest king of Israel. He was the son of King David.
He wrote many psalms and proverbs and
built the temple in Jerusalem.

Homer wrote two famous poems about war and the life of a soldier.

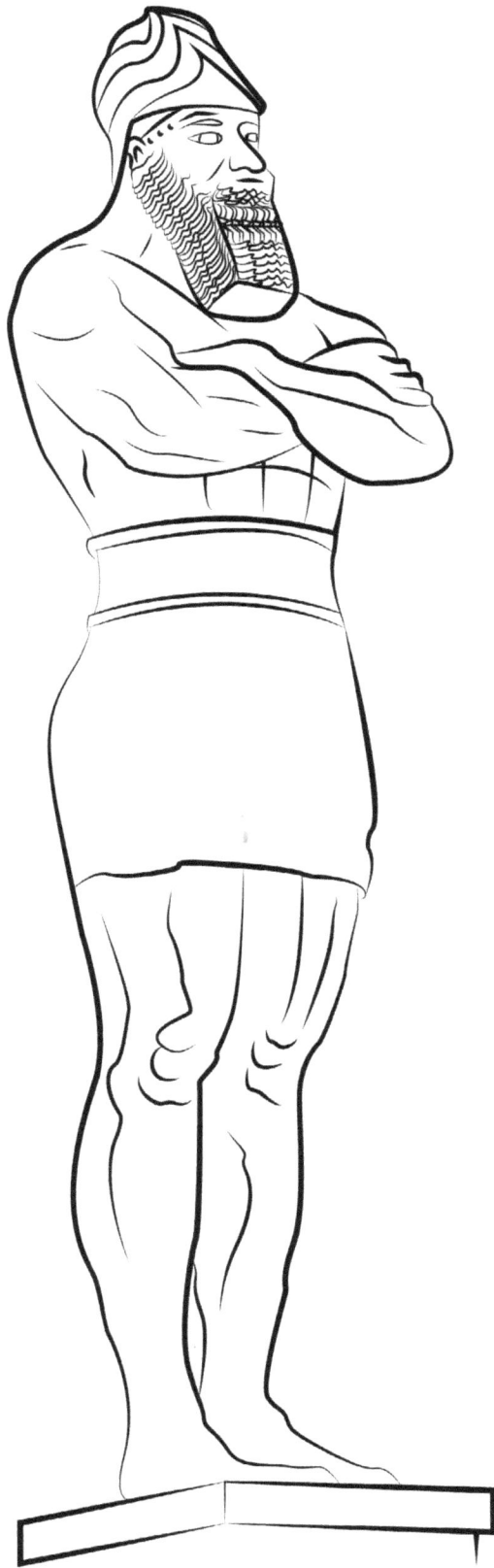

Nebuchadnezzar II was king of Babylon. He created a large statue of himself and wanted everyone to bow down to it.

Thales was one of the Seven Sages of Greece.
He was very smart and loved math.

Daniel loved God. When the king said no one should pray, Daniel continued to pray. The king threw Daniel into the lions' den. But God shut up the mouths of the lions and Daniel was not hurt.

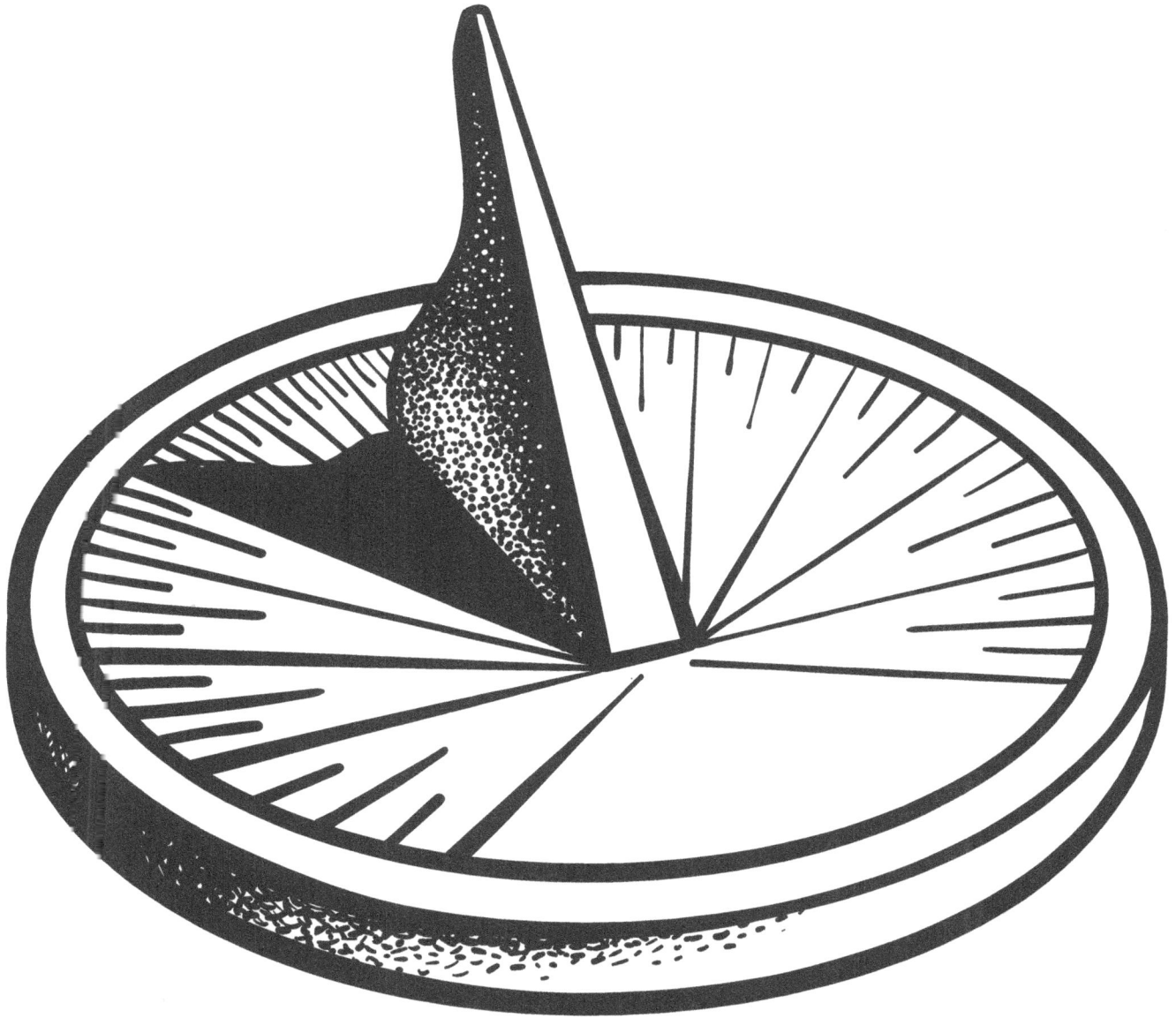

Anaximander of Miletus loved math and science.
He made the sundail to be able to tell time.

Cyrus the Great was the first Persian king.
He helped the Jews rebuild Jerusalem.

Anaximenes of Miletus was a scientist who thought everything was made of air. The Anaximenes crater on the Moon is named in his honor.

$$a^2 + b^2 = c^2$$

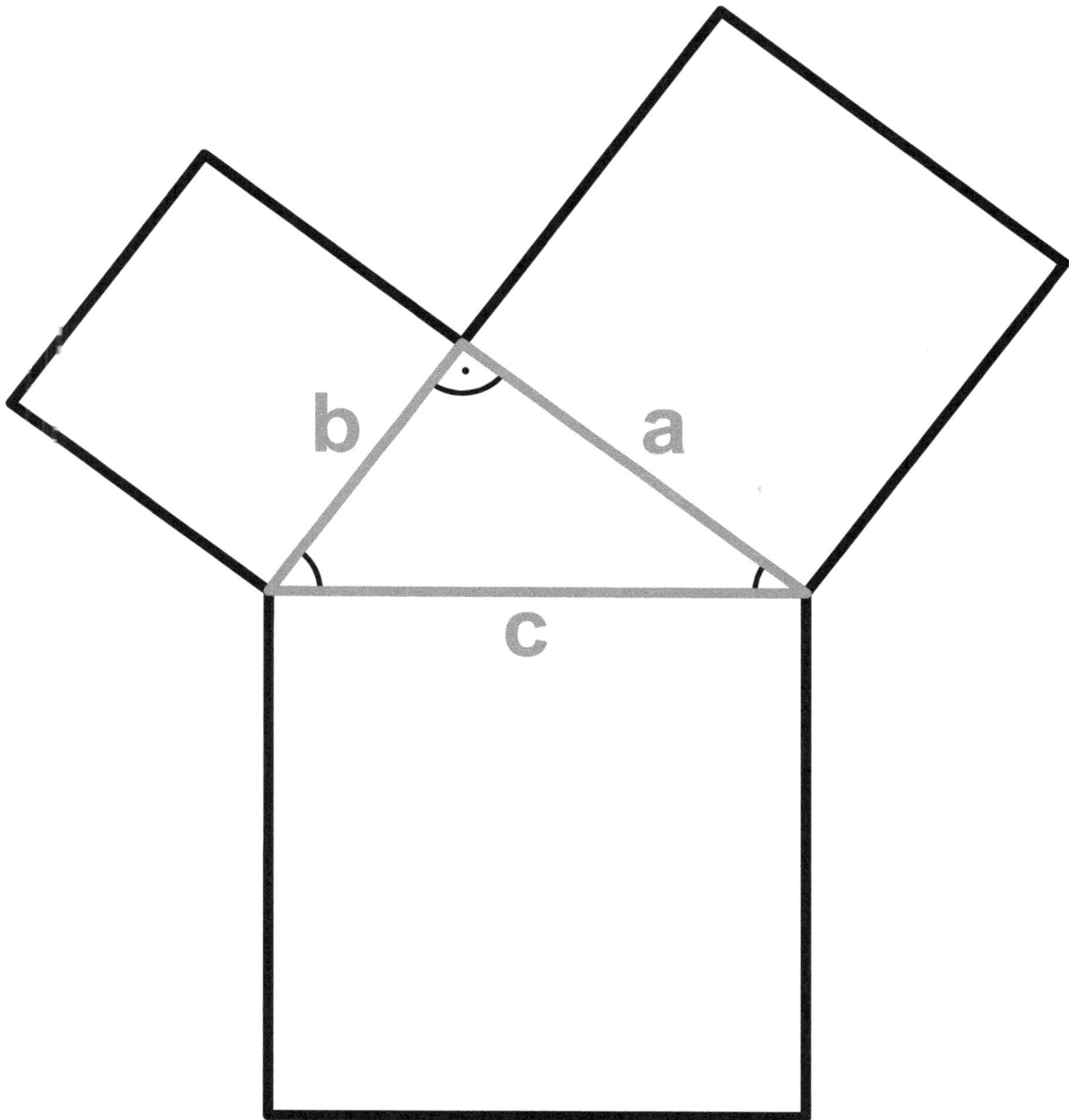

Pythagoras of Samos loved math and astonomy.
He is famous for this:
$a^2 + b^2 = c^2$

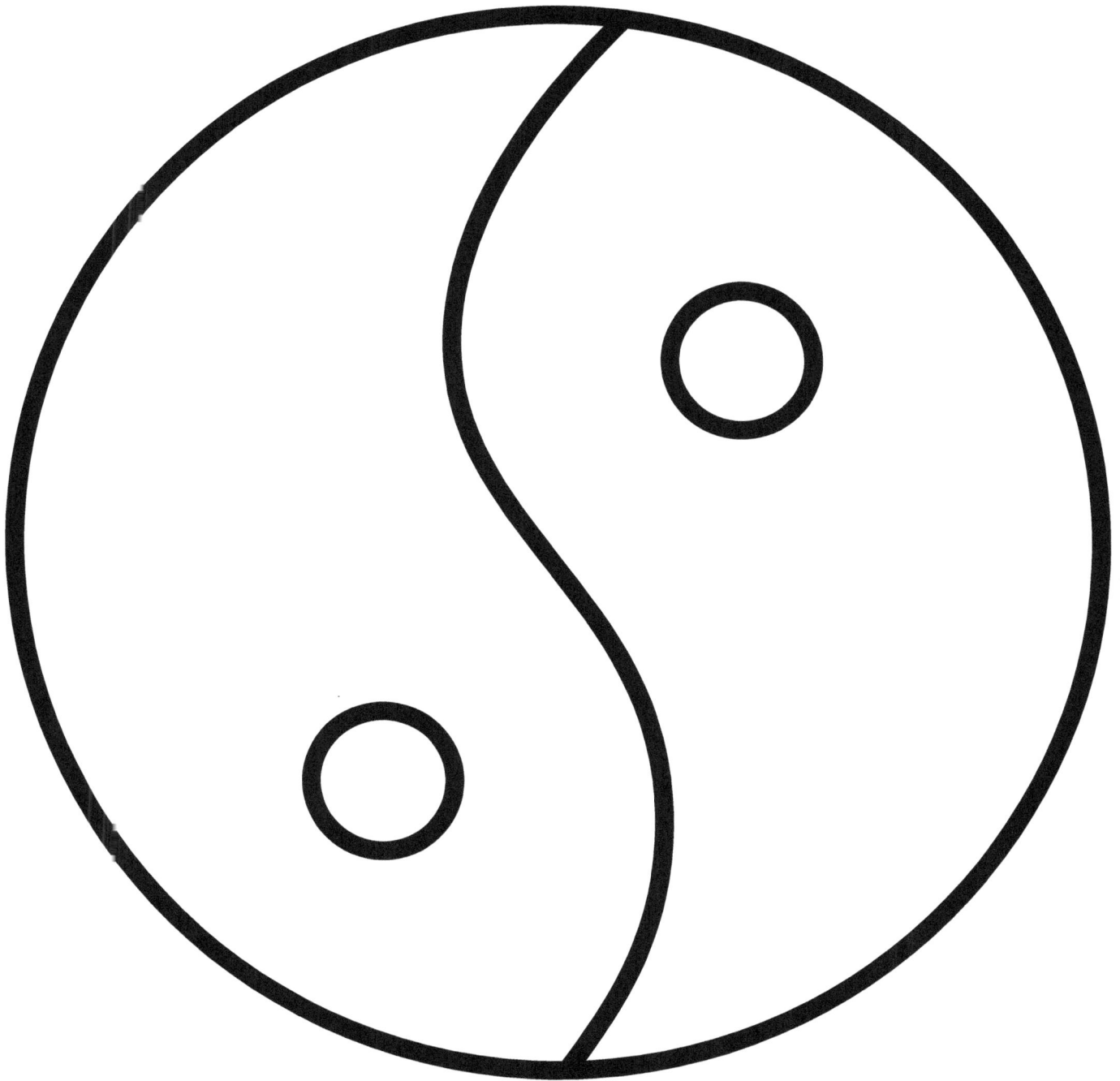

Lao Tzu or Laozi was an ancient Chinese philosopher and writer.
He started a religion called Taoism.

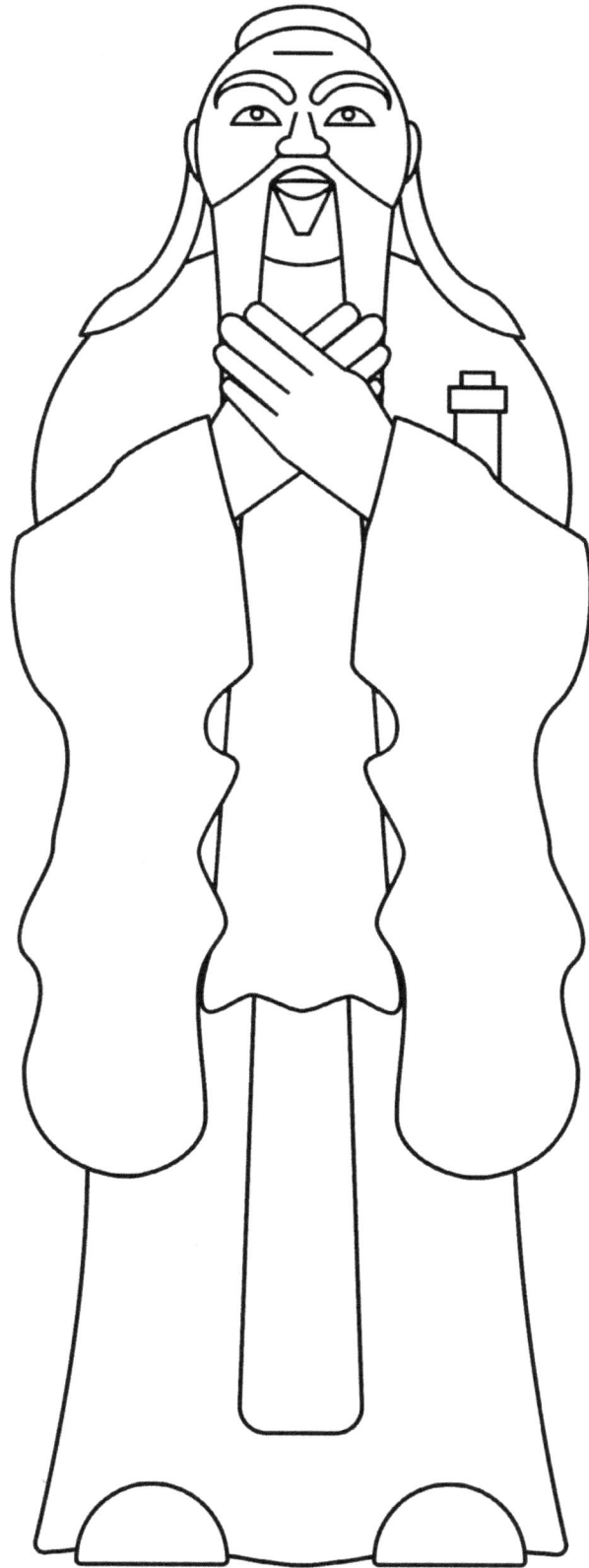

Confucius was a Chinese teacher, editor, politician, and philosopher.
His teaching is known as Confucianism.

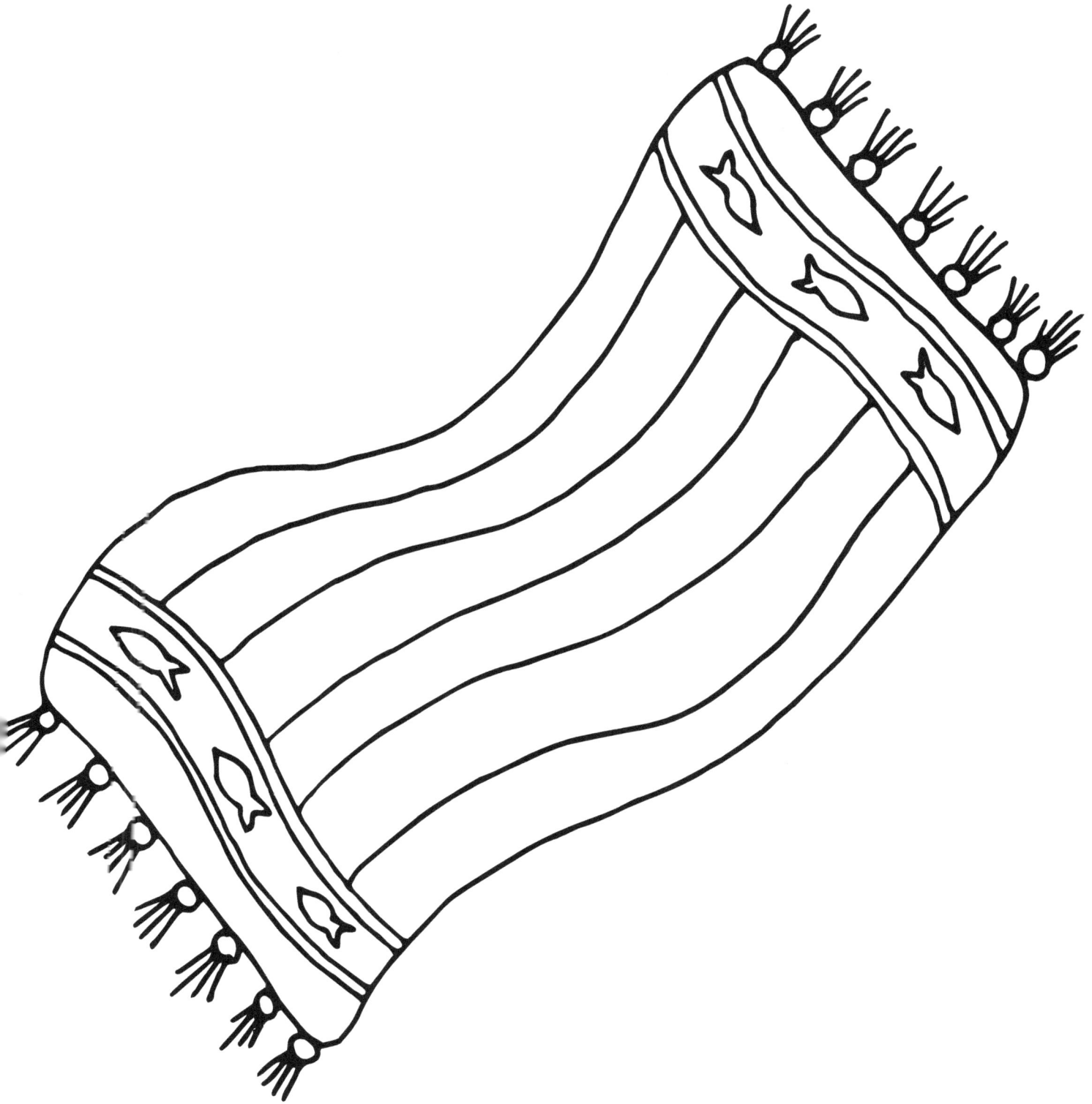

Darius the Great was the fourth king of Persia.
He built roads, buildings, and entire cities.
Persia is known for their colorful carpets.

Buddha was a teacher.
His teachings formed a religion called Buddhism.

Xerxes the Great was a king of Persia and later was Pharoah of Egypt. Some people think he is also Ahasuerus in the biblical Book of Esther.

Esther or Hadassah was a Jewish queen of the Persian king Ahasuerus (possibly Xerxes the Great). Esther was chosen for her beauty. Esther ended up saving the lives of the Jewish people living in Persia.